FIFTY
MYSTERIOUS
POSTCARDS

FIFTY
MYSTERIOUS
POSTCARDS

PITMAN SHORTHAND
MESSAGES FROM
THE GOLDEN AGE
OF THE POSTCARD

KATHRYN BAIRD

First published 2022

The History Press
97 St George's Place, Cheltenham,
Gloucestershire, GL50 3QB
www.thehistorypress.co.uk

British Library Cataloguing in Publication Data.
A catalogue record for this book is available from the British Library.

ISBN 978 1 80399 046 0

Typesetting and origination by The History Press
Printed in Turkey by Imak

CONTENTS

INTRODUCTION

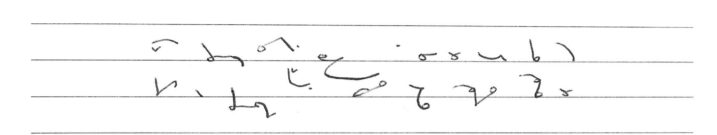

Straight lines, curved lines, short lines, long lines, circles, ticks, hooks, dots and dashes. What is the message in this mysterious code? A declaration of undying love? Arrangements for a clandestine meeting? A newsy message to a penfriend? Scandalous gossip? Without the skill of writing and transcribing Pitman shorthand, the enigma remains. This book takes you on a journey of discovery that begins with setting eyes on an impregnable message, written in shorthand on a postcard many years ago, and ends on its 'big reveal'.

Millions of postcards were sent in the early twentieth century – a period known as the 'Golden Age' of the picture postcard, which stretched roughly from 1900 to 1918. Sending a postcard was the equivalent of texting today. As heads are now bent over mobile phones, so heads were bent over postcards as writers' pencils scribbled away. A short message could be written quickly on a postcard, popped into a postbox and received the next day, such was the reliability of the postal service in those days. In fact, I have some postcards in my collection which reveal the writer's expectation that they will be delivered later that same day. For example, a message sent in 1904 reads, 'This is to remind you that I shall be waiting patiently at the Hammersmith station tonight at 7.45.' A time of extraordinary trust thanks to multiple daily deliveries of post.

Many of these messages written in shorthand held secrets that the sender was at pains to hide from postmen, servants or anyone else living at the recipient's address. Of course, for the strategy to work, the person receiving the postcard had to be able to understand shorthand too. Bearing in mind that no writer uses perfect shorthand outlines, it is not surprising that frequently a part of the message was along the lines of, 'Hope you can read the shorthand.'

Another benefit for the shorthand writer was the small space it required. The space left for writing a message on a postcard is necessarily limited, but it is amazing how much detail can fit into such a small area. Sometimes writing on the front of the postcard as well as the back, a message written in shorthand allowed the sender to include much more detail about their holiday experience or seemingly inconsequential ramblings. An example of a sender getting a lot off his chest is this, from a postcard in my collection, written in 1906:

I felt very unhappy after I left you last night because I didn't know if I had done or said anything that made you feel miserable. I do hope I have not, dear, and I also hope that you feel happier today. You must not think about things that make you miserable or else we shall be having you ill darling. I cannot bear to think that you are worried about anything.

When I first bought a postcard with a message written in shorthand, I was enchanted. I could use my Pitman shorthand skill for something other than work! The message came alive as I read it and my journey into this obscure hobby began. My collection of postcards with mysterious messages has grown slowly since I made that first purchase nearly forty years ago.

The images on the postcards can be fascinating in themselves. I particularly enjoy poring over seaside scenes, complete with Edwardian families wearing their Sunday best while enjoying the beach. Crowds of holidaymakers walk along promenades and piers, some pushing large perambulators. A postcard of the pier at Eastbourne in my collection, posted in 1903, has this revealing message:

I have not been for any steamer trips or drives up till now; we have spent all our time on the seafront. They have motor buses here, so I suggested to mother the other day we should have a ride in one but she did not seem to relish the idea at all. You would almost have thought that I had asked her to go up in a balloon.

Collecting postcards in the 'Golden Age' was a hugely popular hobby, with some people focussing on collecting by theme. Postcards featuring actresses, pictured in costumes from their productions, were highly sought after. One of my postcards has a coloured image of Nina Sevening and this message written in Pitman: 'I hope you will like this actress. Had I known you liked them I would have sent you some before. How is your collection progressing? Mine has been growing gradually of late.'

For some collectors the goal was quantity, rather than collecting specific subjects. One sender, on a postcard sent in 1904, wrote: 'I have now just over 500 cards. How many have you? Several more I expect.'

'Wow!' is a common reaction I hear when somebody sees the postcards in my collection with their squiggly messages. The expectation is of an intimate declaration and, occasionally, this is the case. Here is an example from a postcard of 22 December 1903: 'I respect you darling infinitely and I am sure while we are separated at Christmas you will think of me long and lovingly. I am looking forward so intensely to tomorrow night. I must give vent to my feelings then and I am sure you will feel like me.'

The postcards were frequently kept in albums, to be shown to visiting friends and family, until those heady days of frantic collecting ceased. In 1918, the rate for inland postage doubled to 1*d* and the craze for picture postcards diminished. Safely stored away, many were only to see the light of day again as part of a house clearance. Out of those long-ago-cherished postcards, the ones with messages in shorthand must have caused people to wonder about the secrets they held.

When I see a postcard with a message in shorthand, I first have to make sure I can read it. I am not able to read Teeline or Gregg, both of which are very different from Pitman, so I never purchase those. There are also styles of shorthand that have their roots in Pitman and, at a quick glance, look as if I could transcribe them. I have felt disappointed on the rare occasions when I have tried to read a message written in these unfamiliar codes.

The writers also often turned the postcard upside down or sideways. You will notice this in many of the postcards in this book. So, with the message turned to the correct orientation, I start a quick transcription. How quick depends on many factors. Nobody's shorthand is perfect. Sometimes it is abysmal, although it is always possible to read at least a few outlines, and I have to ask a friend to help me transcribe the most head-scratchingly challenging postcard messages. It helps if the context is clear, but often this is not the case. Many postcards did not make the grade when I was choosing examples for this book because of numerous gaps in transcription.

My hobby is a long way from my early encounters with shorthand. I well remember my first lesson in Pitman New Era shorthand in September 1972. I was enrolled on a two-year medical secretarial course at a further education college. My shorthand and typewriting tutor, Mrs Hill, strode into the classroom and got down to business immediately. No second was wasted in her chalk-and-talk lessons.

Forget spelling; Pitman shorthand is phonetic. For the shorthand writer, the goal is to hear a sound and write it as quickly as possible. Common words must be written automatically, and less familiar words have to be written with a minimum of thought.

Learning the theory – and there is a lot of it – goes hand in hand with writing progressively faster. As Mrs Hill used to say, 'Speed from the beginning; theory to the end.'

By the end of the first lesson, we could all write the first six consonant outlines – 'p', 'b', 't', 'd', 'ch', 'j' – and had started to use our first Pitman vowel sign, a heavy dot to represent the long vowel 'a'. By the end of that first action-packed Pitman lesson, Mrs Hill had taught us to read and write the Pitman outlines for 'ape', 'pay', 'Abe', 'bay', 'aid', 'day' and 'age'. She set us homework that involved more repetition of writing the strokes we had learnt. There was no doubt that learning shorthand demanded serious commitment. I loved it from the beginning.

My first job as a medical secretary was in a large hospital in Liverpool, where I took dictation from consultants and their junior medical staff every day. I would sit with my shorthand notebook resting on my knee, pencil poised, and then type up clinic letters on an old, green, sit-up-and-beg Imperial typewriter. The shorthand was, of course, a means to an end. I found myself using it to make quick notes to myself out of work, but it was firmly associated in my mind with my secretarial job.

A few years later, I went back to college for evening classes and qualified as a teacher of shorthand. While I can no longer pretend that I remember all the Pitman New Era rules and explanations for them, in 1977 I could confidently reel off such niche concepts as advanced phraseography using the doubling principle, when to use 'stroke -ing' and when to use 'dot -ing', and use of the medial semicircle. All meaningless to those who know nothing of shorthand and puzzling to those who learnt to write shorthand a long time ago.

In 1982 I started training to teach 'office arts', more commonly known as secretarial studies, in further and higher education. It was a time of technological change in offices, with the introduction of word processors and more reliance on audio typing than shorthand typing. Pitman New Era, with which I was so familiar, had been introduced in 1922 and was widely taught in the UK. But a streamlined version called Pitman 2000, which was quicker to learn due to fewer rules and simplified outlines, was published in 1975. I found myself teaching both Pitman New Era and 2000 – the two versions used by Pitmanites today. But Teeline, a system developed in 1968, based on spelling rather than phonetics, is now more widely taught and used in the UK.

Shorthand was originally known as phonography ('sound writing'). Isaac Pitman published his first pamphlet in 1837, named 'Stenographic Sound-Hand', and spent the next three years improving the system beyond recognition. In 1840, this revised edition appeared called *Phonography, or Writing by Sound, being also a New and Natural System of Shorthand*. In 1857, the tenth edition of Pitman's *Phonography* was published and, over the rest of the inventor's life, he made many more changes. Pitman was not alone in devising a shorthand system. There was a plethora of systems created and used, particularly in the late nineteenth century, most of which are now lost in the mists of time.

The shorthand on the postcards in this book are written in pre-New Era versions of Pitman. Although the basic outlines are the same, there are subtle differences and over time, I have become adept at transcribing them. Shorthand writers frequently make up their own outlines to the point where they are only loosely based on the rules of Pitman shorthand. This is not a problem in a work situation where the writer is the one to read their own shorthand and transcribe it. But what if a Pitmanite writes a shorthand message to somebody else, for example, on a holiday postcard? Their shorthand may be beautifully, heart-warmingly accurate or it could be appallingly incorrect.

For many years, I kept my hobby a secret. I didn't know anybody else who collected postcards, let alone postcards with shorthand messages. I squirrelled my collection away and didn't think about it until I had another one to add to it. But in 2017, I started my Twitter account (@Kathryn11Baird) and frequently tweeted a little shorthand, sometimes from the postcards in my collection. Popular with those who have no knowledge of shorthand as well as Pitmanites, the postcards provide a fascinating little glimpse of the use of a dying art.

Remember my shorthand message to you at the start of this introduction? Perhaps you understand Pitman and have already transcribed it. Or maybe the mysterious squiggles have left you wondering about its coded message. The wait is over:

My postcard hobby is no longer a secret. Now it is your turn to discover the tiny stories of these mysterious messages.

THE FIRST OF MANY

In 1983, my exhausting first-year timetable featured me teaching Pitman 2000 to a beginners' evening class alongside typewriting, office practice and a unit on the medical secretarial course about social services and the NHS. Always looking for creative ways to interest my students, I started collecting old postcards of hospitals to help with my teaching of the history of the health service.

At that time, I read that some old postcards had messages written in code, such as Morse or shorthand. Without too much enthusiasm, as my main interest was in hospitals, I asked dealers if they had any postcards with messages in shorthand. It took many visits to postcard fairs before I found one of Hubberholme Church, near Buckden in Yorkshire, posted in 1905, with a message in Pitman shorthand. On the front, I read the message: 'I am coming home on Sunday afternoon.'

But it was the message on the reverse that got me hooked.

Dear Madge,

I am at present on my holidays. Have not heard from you lately. How are you getting on? I am writing this in shorthand because they always read what is on postcards at the post office here. This is the church I was at on Sunday night.

Kindest regards from Annie Tennant

HUBBERHOLME CHURCH, near BUCKDEN.   Grimshawe's Upper Wharfedale Series.

MANOR HOUSE,
BUCKDEN.
SKIPTON. POST ● CARD.

YORKS.

11-80

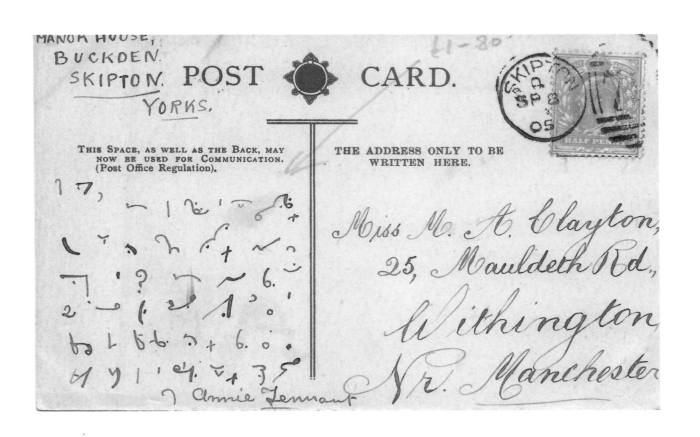

Annie Tennant

Miss M. A. Clayton,
25, Mauldeth Rd.,
Withington,
Nr. Manchester

SKIPTON
SP 8
05

HALF PENNY

PENFRIENDS

Postcard collectors in the 'Golden Age' of the postcard often advertised for pen-friends. Those who could read and write Pitman sometimes sought penfriends who also wished to write their messages in shorthand to add interest to their collections.

Albert Wells sent postcards from the Isle of Wight, where he was a patient at an open-air hospital, to his penfriend Mr Smith. This one of Pond, Bonchurch, sent in 1903, explains his situation in regard to corresponding with other penfriends. The message begins on the front:

My dear Mr Smith.

Your pretty card to hand yesterday for which please accept my best thanks. Yes I got a lot of replies to my advertisement but the reason I am not corresponding with anyone now is because I have not got much time as it is rather hard to write when out of doors — it takes nearly all my time to write home and to several of my friends. But I shall <u>always</u> be pleased to write to you. I am much better again today and I hope I will continue to get better. I thank you sincerely for your kind wishes. We are having splendid weather here and it looks like continuing. With kindest regards

From yours sincerely
A Wells

Pond.   Bonchurch I. o. W.

POST CARD – GREAT BRITAIN & IRELAND

THE ADDRESS ONLY TO BE WRITTEN ON THIS SIDE.

A. H. S. Smith Esq
190 Gorton Rd
Reddish
Stockport

The front of this postcard of Westminster Abbey, London, posted on 31 October 1903, features a 106-word message in precise, tiny shorthand from Lionel Wimpenny. He clearly wanted to fit in as long a message as possible and to be sure that the recipient could read it:

WESTMINSTER ABBEY, LONDON.

Dear Sir,

Many thanks for your card which I was pleased to receive. I note that you are interested in picture cards and I shall be pleased to exchange some with you. I have only recently started collecting and have about 100 at present. I like the view you sent me and I hope you will like the above! Yes! I agree with you and think it is very interesting and it gives you an idea as to what certain places are like so you can make up your mind where to spend your holiday if you are in doubt as to where to go to!

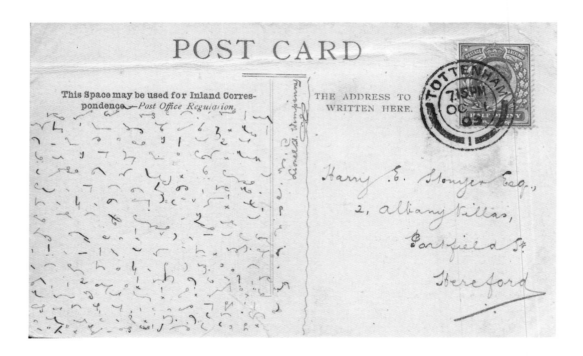

Even more impressive is the 260-word message on the reverse. It reveals that Lionel and Henry have recently started corresponding as 'shorthand penfriends'. The formal tone is surprising nowadays but not unusual for the time. I have no idea what Lionel means with his reference to 'Joe': a mystery waiting to be solved.

I am pleased to learn that you are willing to correspond with me, and of course it need not be entirely conducted on picture postcards unless we choose to do so. I have found it very good practice myself as since I do not do any shorthand in the office now I do not get so much practice as formerly. I have no doubt that our correspondence will be mutually beneficial. Thanks for your kindness in offering to get me some Japanese stamps but I am afraid I haven't the time to devote to stamp collecting that I should like! Nevertheless, please accept my best thanks for your kindness and I shall be pleased to accept any which your friend may be able to send you! I was to go in for photography but had to give it up owing to lack of time. I am sorry to say nearly all my spare time is devoted to study so I cannot say what is my hobby, but shorthand certainly is! I am also very fond of drawing but I am afraid I have too many irons in the fire! Yes! You are quite right as to the "physical" question – I am interested in it, but when you once get started on it you never know when to stop. I may say therefore that I am a failure to "Joe". I think we could correspond on general matters if that would suit you.

Trusting to have the pleasure of hearing from you again soon, I remain,
yours faithfully
Lionel H Wimpenny

Southampton.   The Avenue.

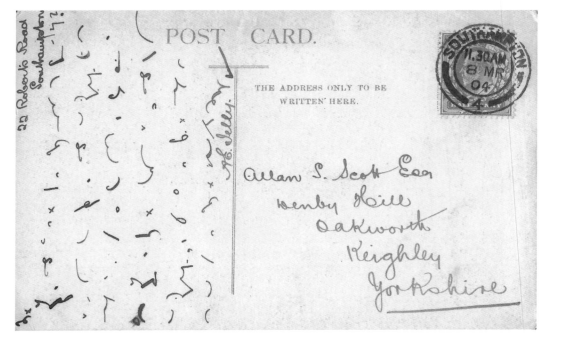

POST CARD.

THE ADDRESS ONLY TO BE
WRITTEN HERE.

22 Roberts Road
Southampton
24-7-?2

Allan S. Scott Esq
Denby Hill
Oakworth
Keighley
Yorkshire

A postcard of The Avenue, Southampton, from Archibald E. Jelly records the start of correspondence with a penfriend in 1904:

22 Roberts Road, Southampton
Dear Sir,
  I shall be pleased to correspond with you. Do you prefer coloured or black and white?
I should like if possible to correspond in Esperanto though my knowledge of the language
is very limited but for the sake of self-improvement I shall be glad to do so. If you like I
would correspond by letter in Esperanto, but just as you please. Kindly let me know
which you prefer.
  Awaiting reply
  Yours very truly
  A E Jelly

Guildhall, London.

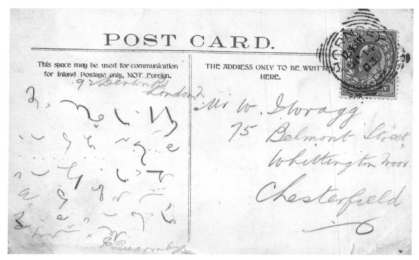

Collections of hundreds of postcards were not unusual and penfriends were eager to exchange views of places:

92 Denton Road, London 2.
Dear Sir.
    Your very nice view of Derbyshire to hand for which I thank you and I herewith send you in exchange a view of the Guildhall London for which I trust you will like, and shall be glad to send you any further views which you may like.
    Yours truly
    J A Quarmby

HOLIDAYS

Many of the postcards were sent by holidaymakers. The postcard below shows a rather alarming retreat from the incoming tide in Douglas, Isle of Man. Its message is typical of the holiday postcard sent from one shorthand writer to another:

Dear Bert

Having a glorious time, fine every day. We have faces like potted lobsters and the skin is peeling off. Jim would tell you we had come to the Isle of Man. I never saw you to tell you. We shall be stopping till next Wednesday.
Yours faithfully,
Martin Hyde

The expectation of sending and receiving holiday postcards is clear from this message on a postcard of Exeter Cathedral sent in 1917:

Dear Rene

Just a couple of lines from this place as you so kindly remembered me when you were away. We have so far had a glorious time and have been able to see a number of interesting places. We have not yet made up our minds where we will spend tomorrow but expect to leave here in the morning. We have had to run about a good deal and have walked about 14 miles today but it has been worth the effort.
This must be all just now.
With kind regards I am your sincere friend
Ralph Johnson.

EXETER CATHEDRAL. — North Side. — LL.

Published by Worth and Co., Exeter.

POST CARD

Inlar.d ½ d.

Foreign 1 d.

Printed in France

Penzance 5/8/17

Barnard Castle attained a certain notoriety during the Covid-19 pandemic, but this postcard shows its popularity as a holiday destination in 1906:

Galgate, Barnard Castle.

25/17

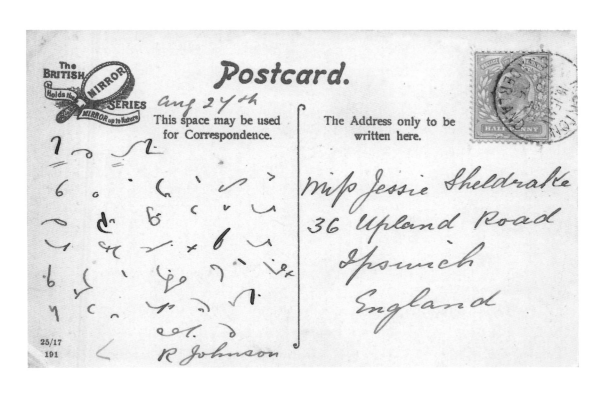

Postcard.

The BRITISH MIRROR SERIES
Holds the MIRROR up to Nature

Aug 27th

This space may be used for Correspondence.

The Address only to be written here.

HALF PENNY

Miss Jessie Sheldrake
36 Upland Road
Ipswich
England

25/17
191

R Johnson

Dear Miss Sheldrake

This is a view of one of the most beautiful places that I know in the north country. Just now it is full of visitors from all parts. I hope that you enjoyed your holiday.

Sincerely yours
R Johnson

Tiny shorthand meant that the writer of this postcard from the Clifton Observatory in Bristol was able to tell his parents a lot of detail about his holiday jaunts in 1913. A little research reveals that the sender's full name was Charles Richard Probert, but the Pitman outline for his name reads as Carl. Names can be particularly tricky to transcribe because Pitman is phonetic and does not give clues about spelling. You will find a second postcard from the same person in the 'First World War' chapter, where he writes his name in longhand as Carlie.

This is lovely Pitman shorthand, written using a lot of the dots and dashes that indicate vowels, making it easy to transcribe. If only all shorthand messages were written as accurately!

Bristol
8/2/13
1.45 pm
Dear father and mother,

I am having a splendid time here. Last night I went to the Hippodrome with Bertie and saw the best music hall show I have ever seen. This morning, as it was finer than yesterday, I went out with Trixie on the trams, etc to Clifton and Durdham Downs. We saw the Bridge and Observatory. We went into the latter and explored a cave in the cliffs and saw a third class Camera Obscura. This afternoon I suppose I shall be going out again. Tonight I anticipate going to the pantomime. I am beginning to know my way about a little bit better, but I have not been able to get a Borough guide yet. Best love to you again. I will write more fully tomorrow if I get a chance.
Carl

The Observatory   Clifton Down

POST CARD

Printed in Great Britain

This space may be used for Communication   The Address to be written

BRISTOL

11. 30 PM
8 FEB 13A

"Bee" Series, Burgess & Co., Bristol & W. S. Ltd.

8/2/13.
1·45 P.M.

Mr & Mrs C. A. Probert,

58, Brighton Road,

Cheltenham.

Sometimes the sender was keen to know of events back home, as in this postcard of Carisbrooke Castle on the Isle of Wight, sent in 1909:

CARISBROOKE CASTLE, I.W.

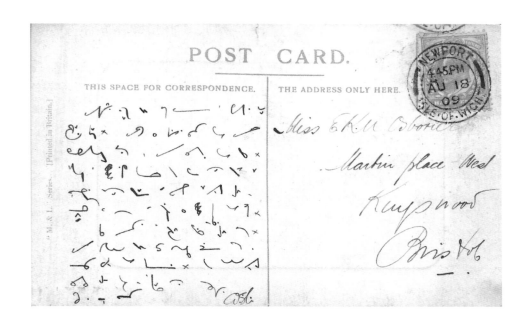

We duly arrived about 7 o'clock on Saturday night frightfully tired. Weather is turning slightly for the worst since we have been here but we are hoping for the best. I have had a saddle fixed up for my boy on the cross-bar of my bike and yesterday I rode down to Cowes with him and paddled his tooties in the water.

It is really a beautiful place down here. We are living about 5 minutes' walk from the castle shown in the picture. If anything rotten happens don't fail to advise me. There's a good girl.

Yours truly, *

Fitting a long message in the small space of a postcard is a doddle when it is written in Pitman shorthand. I wonder whether Fred could read everything written to him by Frank on this postcard of Feather's Plain and Free Library, Gorleston, in 1913. The shorthand is squashed together at the end and the postmark obscures part of it. One word has escaped my transcription, indicated by an asterisk.

Dear Fred

Thanks for postcard. I am afraid we shall not be able to stay after Saturday as our rooms are let again much as I should like to have seen you all. We have just come back from a bathe. The sea is beautiful here and so safe for bathing. There is a diver working in the harbour and we have seen him going down twice. It is very peculiar and amusing to see him dress. I think he will be here next week. I should like to have stayed a day or so longer and have had a chat with you but you know the attractions here are many and funds of course run low after a couple of weeks. I can only wish that you will have a good time as I believe you will. The weather I think will be fine. We had a sea trip last night round the Saint Nicholas light ship. We shall be leaving by the 1.20 train on Saturday so am afraid we shall not be able to say * That's the fast train to London.

Kind regards to all

Frank

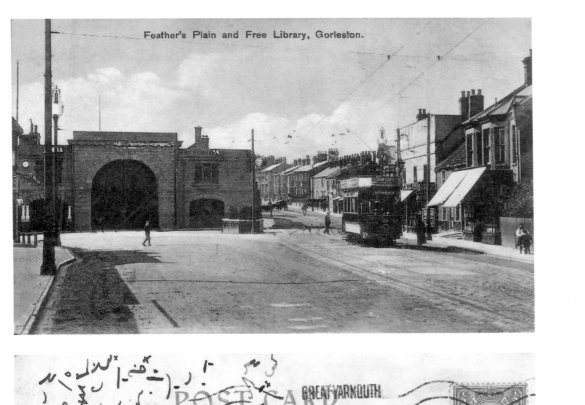

Feather's Plain and Free Library, Gorleston.

GREAT YARMOUTH
3. —M
14 AUG 13

Mr. F. W. Tucker
37 Salisbury Rd
Walthamstow
Essex

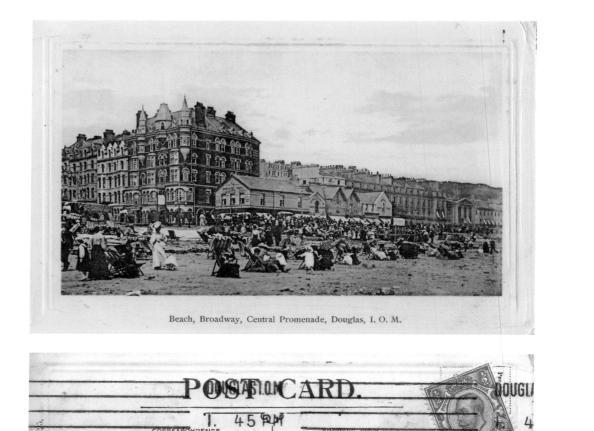

Beach, Broadway, Central Promenade, Douglas, I. O. M.

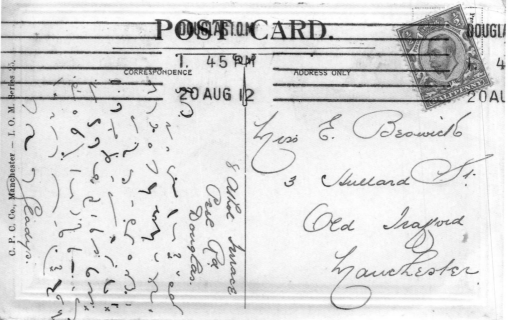

POST CARD.

CORRESPONDENCE

ADDRESS ONLY

C. P. C. Co., Manchester — I. O. M. Series 25.

Miss E. Beswick
3 Mullard St.
Old Trafford
Manchester

The journey to the holiday destination could be an adventure in itself, and not necessarily a pleasant one, as described in this postcard from the Isle of Man in 1912 to Lizzie Beswick. I have a small collection of postcards sent to Lizzie and you will find several others later in this book.

8 Athol Terrace, Peel Road, Douglas
Dear Lizzie
How are you feeling by now? I sincerely hope your throat is much better and that you are better in yourself.
We arrived here quite safely as you will see but had a very rough passage and were all ill even Dad. Weather has been very nice so far but it is raining this morning. The sun is just peeping out now so perhaps it is going to clear up. How are your mother and father? Both well I hope.
Much love from Gladys

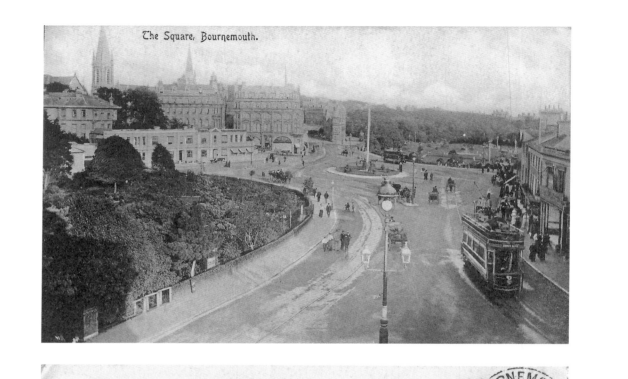

The Square, Bournemouth.

POST CARD.

This space may be used for inland
communication only.

The address only to be
written here.

F. W. King & Co's, Artistic Series, Copyright, No 3017

BOURNEMOUTH
5.45 PM
AU 14
06

HALF PENNY

Miss M. G. Hole
40, St. Johns Rd
Neaville

keeler

The picture postcard of The Square, Bournemouth, sent in 1906, shows the horse-drawn transport and tram common for the time in this popular seaside resort. The formality of the message is not unusual.

I am having a very good time here and fairly good weather. We had a little rain yesterday afternoon. I am coming home on Friday and shall return to business on Monday morning. Kind regards.
    Yours faithfully M.E.S.

WRITING SHORTHAND

Many shorthand messages on postcards include an understandable concern that the reader might not be able to read it. Pitman shorthand is usually written on lined paper, and whether an outline starts above the line, on the line or through the line indicates the first vowel in the word. With the absence of these helpful lines, transcription can be challenging.

Special shorthand pens were commonly used at the time and writers sometimes blamed their pen for less-than-perfect shorthand. This postcard of Tamworth Castle has a short but pithy message, written in ink, by somebody whose name escapes my transcription:

Dear Babs,
    Hope you are having a nice holiday. We are getting on very nicely without you.
Would not have you at any price.
    Hope you will be able to read this, I cannot make thin strokes with this pen.
Much love, *

Tamworth Castle

38810. IV.

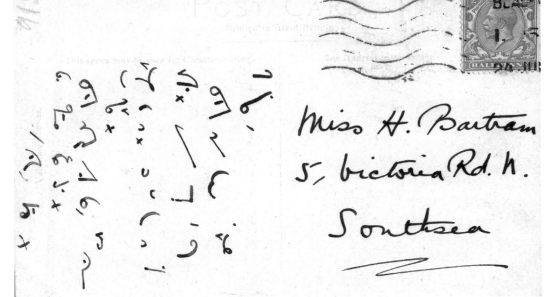

HALF

Miss H. Bartram
5, Victoria Rd. N.
Southsea

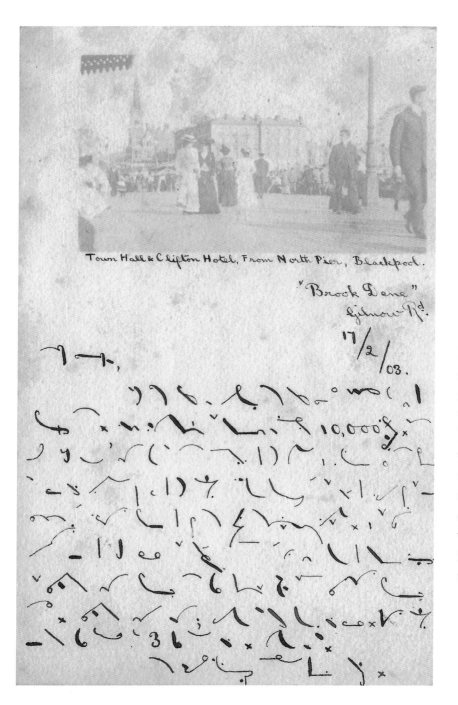

Town Hall & Clifton Hotel, From North Pier, Blackpool.

"Brook Dene"
Gillmow Rd.
17/2/03.

It is rare to find such clear shorthand as written on this real photographic postcard of the town hall and Clifton Hotel, Blackpool. This is beautifully written Pitman and, although not always technically correct, the writer makes good use of dots and dashes to indicate vowels where they are needed for the reader to make sense of the message.

"Brook Dene"
Gilnow Road
17/2/03

My dear Gertrude,

I was very pleased to receive your postcard as I almost thought you had forgotten me. About the album I beg you to accept 10,000 apologies. I am sure I don't know what you will think of me keeping it so long but the fact is my stock of gold paint ran out when it was only half finished and I put it away till I got some more and completely forgot it till your gentle reminder arrived. But I will really get it done as soon as I possibly can and let you have it back again. I hope you will forgive me this time although I can hardly forgive myself. Hope you are all well; we have all been having bad colds. Dolly only got up this afternoon after 3 days in bed. Love to all.

Your always affectionate cousin Dick Paiton.

Reproduced from an original F. Frith & Co. postcard.

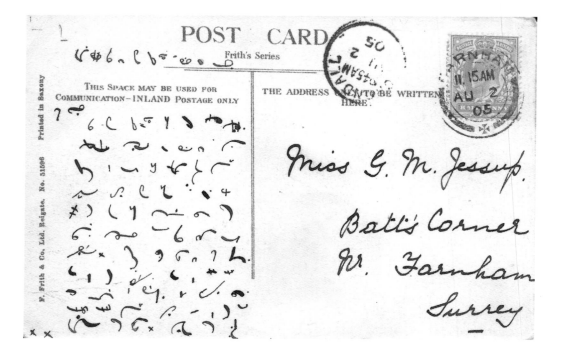

On this postcard of Farnham, posted in 1905, Edith blames illness for the possibility of mistakes in her shorthand:

Phil thanks you for postcard and sends two kisses.

Dear Grace

   Thanks for postcard. I had been meaning to send you a letter before but now I don't feel like writing one for I have a bad cold so if I do make some very silly mistakes in this you will know the reason. Percy says will you tell Jim that he was sorry that he couldn't come on Sunday but the weather seemed like rain and he was not feeling very well.

   Love from Edith xx

ARDEN HALL, HAINNEL

42

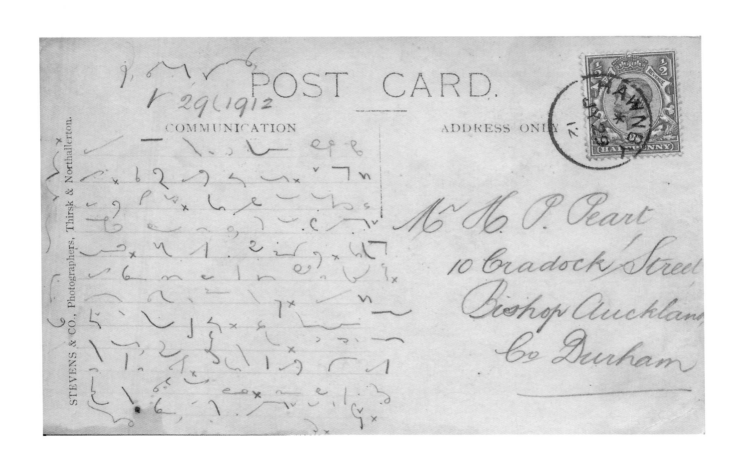

POST CARD.

COMMUNICATION

ADDRESS ONLY

STEVENS & CO., Photographers, Thirsk & Northallerton.

Mr H. P. Peart
10 Cradock Street
Bishop Auckland
Co Durham

43

Ernest Peart, who sent the postcard of Arden Hall, Hawnby, to his brother Henry in 1912, served in the Royal Army Service Corps in the First World War. Ernest's short-hand and typewriting were recorded in his military record as being 'Very Good'. He drew lines on this postcard so that his impeccably written Pitman could be more easily read. Part of Ernest's address has defied my transcription but, overall, this is excellent shorthand. It seems that the brothers were members of the Independent Order of Rechabites, a friendly society and part of the temperance movement.

At the side of the postcard Ernest has written, 'Put this card in my album.'

*, Hawnby, Helmsley
July 29th 1912

We are going up to east bank as soon as it stops raining. It is very bad weather here now. I got about wet through last night. Have you received any intimation when the extension centre meeting is, or any other Rechabite communications. I have read the Shorthand Weekly through. If you have got one this week you may send it to me as soon as you finish with it. Mother will have to walk up today. We are about tired of being down here. When is the picnic going to be now, seeing that it has been put off. What kind of camp meeting had you yesterday. If you had weather like we had it would have to be held in the schools. You can send out the arrears forms this week, and remember the Rechabite night on Friday.

Ernest

FIRST WORLD WAR

On 31 March 1917, Glen wrote to his father from Tidworth Camp in Wiltshire. I wish I knew more.

31.3.17

Dear father

This is a general view of the camp. We have no definite word as yet as to when we go off but I think it will be some day next week. I am getting fit and well and getting on very well as a corporal. There seem very decent fellows here and I have made quite a number of friends who were quite enthusiastic at my promotion especially the fellows from Didcot.

We have several picture houses here and a theatre which helps to make things more lively.

Trust you are well.

Your son, Glen

S 12624   GENERAL VIEW TIDWORTH. NO. 4.

G 47795. BEDFORD: HIGH STREET.

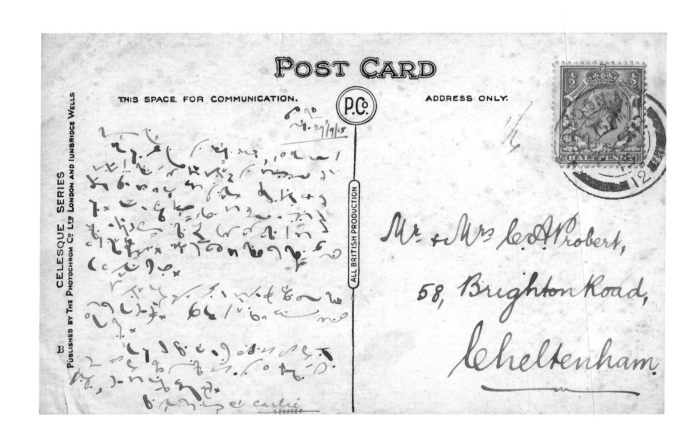

POST CARD

THIS SPACE. FOR COMMUNICATION.   P.C.   ADDRESS ONLY.

CELESQUE SERIES
Published by The Photochrom Co Ltd London and Tunbridge Wells
B

ALL BRITISH PRODUCTION

Mr + Mrs C A Probert,

58, Brighton Road,

Cheltenham.

A postcard of Bedford, sent from Carlie to his parents in 1915, shows soldiers on the High Street, three of them looking out of the window of Bliss Dental Surgery ('Painless Extractions'). This is the second postcard from him; see the first in the 'Holidays' section. Carlie has squeezed a long message onto this postcard and a few outlines are unfortunately indecipherable to me.

Haynes Park
Monday, 27/9/15
Dear mother and father
I have today received father's letter of Sunday afternoon, but as I have nothing much to report at present and little time to reply to that letter I am again making use of a postcard just to let you know that I am still alive. It has been terribly cold here today. Owing to changes at the Gloucester offices I am asking the * people to address the paper to the Cheltenham address and shall be glad if you will kindly re-address it to me when it arrives on Thursday morning. I note your remarks about persons from Bristol and will mention them when replying there next.
I will reply in full to the letter referred to tomorrow (unless something prevents me from doing so). This is the view which I confused with another you mentioned as being pretty.
I have today been placed under two fresh sergeants — one for the cable work and one for the instrument lectures — the latter is telegraphist and also a journalist, so I am * that he may be useful.
Best love from your affectionate son Carlie.

Fairy Glen, Dwygyfylchi.

This postcard of Fairy Glen, Dwygyfylchi, is franked 'Field Post Office 23 Sp 16' and is addressed to a staff sergeant at the Canadian Corps HQ in France. The message starts, 'My dearest husband', so we can expect that this contains a loving message. But does it? There are two outlines which have escaped my transcription.

Dwygyfylchi, Sept 20/16.

My dearest husband,

    We are just here. Have come by train to Llandudno Junction and then walked through Conway across the mountains and through the pass beginning with * and have just had our tea in this village and are now going to view this glen and are then walking to Penmaenmawr. We have two of Annie's friends with us.

    Best and fondest love *

804. Brook in Waterfall Lane

Gordon Smith, Stroud Green Road, N.

POST CARD

WOOD GREEN. N.

8. 30 PM

19 SEP 16

WOOD GREEN. N.

8. 30 PM

19 SEP

Miss M. Cordwell,

4 Hetley Road

Shepherds

Bush,

N.

14 43125

Agnes.

In August 1916, a documentary and propaganda war film named *The Battle of the Somme* was released. Agnes sent a postcard of 'Brook in Waterfall Lane' in the following month and mentions her plan to see this popular film. It sounds as if May, the recipient, is a work colleague.

My dear May.

Just a card to let you know that I am having a fine time. It is a change to get away from him. Are you being worked to death? I hope you are not. The weather is not at all bad but the morning today was vile. Don't you think the war is going on fine? I think it is a treat to read the papers just at present. We went to see Sir George Alexander yesterday and we are going to see The Battle of the Somme on Friday. Will tell you all about it when we meet on Monday.

Much love

Agnes

SWEETHEARTS

The roses on the postcard signify love, as does the angle of the stamp. I hope Queenie was able to read the pencilled message; it's particularly difficult underneath the postmark.

2.9.13

My own darling Queenie

 Well darling I hope you are getting on all right now darling and that you are having better weather than we are. It has been simply disgusting today dear and has rained practically the whole of the day. The boss has been up today but he is in a very good mood and everything went off very well for the first day. He left early and I was home soon after 6.30. I hope darling you are having a jolly time now your mother is with you. There is no need why you should not dear is there. Bye bye darling. Trusting you are keeping well. With all my love, always, Charlie.

Josephine also wrote in pencil on this postcard of Ayton but fortunately it is legible, apart from a name. The card is addressed to Mr G.F. Harrison, but Josephine starts the message, 'My dear', followed by a shorthand outline for the sound 'm'. I wonder what it represents? The top left corner reads, 'Sorry I cannot find a decent place to write a bit more news.'

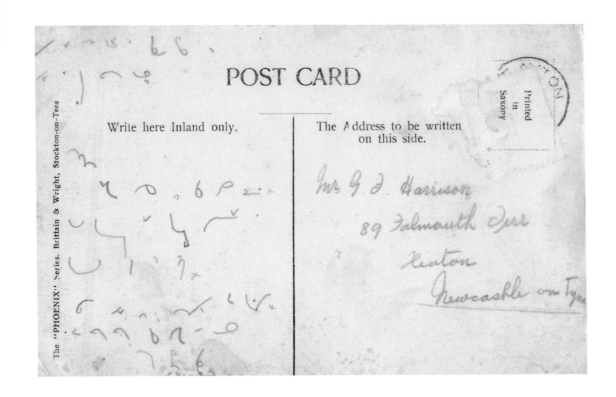

My dear *
    I have missed you this last week. In fact I have been like a fish out of water.
    Will write you tomorrow without fail.
    With very very best love and kisses
    Your sweetheart Josephine

This postcard with a map and poem of Truelove River is postmarked 13 February 1907, so is no doubt a Valentine's message sent in the traditional anonymous way:

> *Dear Nellie,*
> *Accept the kiss contained in this*
> *And let this heart be only thine*
> *This happy day, say, only say*
> *You will be mine sweet valentine.*
> *An admirer*

At the bottom, in pencil, is the reply: 'Yes darling. I will be your sweet valentine.'

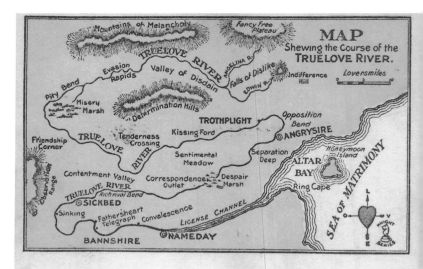

TRUELOVE RIVER.

There's a River old in a land of gold,
  As gossips all relate,
A River whose course, from bar to source,
  Never ran smooth or straight.
And every lass and every lad,
  Once on that stream afloat,
Must thread the maze of its winding ways,
  Till the salt seas rock their boat.
  Refrain :
Misery Marsh and Pity Bend,
  Friendship Corner, the stream runs fast,
Tenderness Crossing, Kissing Ford,
  And Trothplight Town is reached at last.
Oh, Truelove River, give my love to me,
  Honeymoon Isle is over the bar, so carry
  us out to sea.

Full words and Music of the above Song can be had from all Music-dealers and Stationers, or from Knight Brothers, 18, Holborn, London. Words by R. Norman Silver. Music by Herbert E. Haines, part composer of "The Catch of the Season." Over 220,000 copies of "The Map of Truelove River" have been sold.

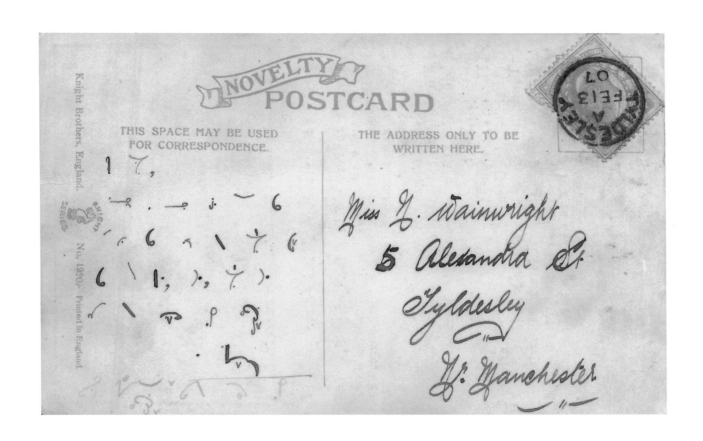

NOVELTY POSTCARD

Knight Brothers, England.

KNIGHT SERIES

No. 1920. Printed in England.

THIS SPACE MAY BE USED
FOR CORRESPONDENCE.

THE ADDRESS ONLY TO BE
WRITTEN HERE.

Miss H. Wainwright
5 Alexandra St.
Tyldesley
Nr. Manchester

On this postcard of actress Agnes Fraser to Lillian, her 'true and devoted boy Harry' has squeezed a very long message in his tiny Pitman shorthand. Although the standard of Harry's outlines is better than most shorthand writers, there are three words that escape me.

My darling sweetheart: I have been thinking sweetheart that it would be just a little bit risky waiting about outside a theatre on Saturday night especially if it is wet or cold – I don't think we ought to chance it so soon after your little illness do you? So I have asked a friend to get me seats for Saturday – either for "Robin Hood" or "The Man From Blankley's". So you must wear your tartan dress, my * And I will wear my * What time to bed last night? Half past 12 again I expect. I shall distinctly have to tell Frank that I disapprove of my girl being kept up so late when she ought to be going to bed early, especially after her cold. Because you know there is nothing like late nights for giving you colds. I am having Wednesday holiday so expect me over fairly early. Then perhaps we can all go for a walk? I stayed till six o'clock tonight and shall stay again tomorrow night – I have such a lot of work to get done before I go down to * I keep thinking today's Tuesday. If only it were! Then I should see my darling tomorrow instead of the day after; so now I can only send my dearest and fondest love – always your own true and devoted boy Harry. Love to all.

PS Do you ever read these?

4067 H ROTARY PHOTO, E.C.   MISS AGNES FRASER.   FOULSHAM & BANFIELD.

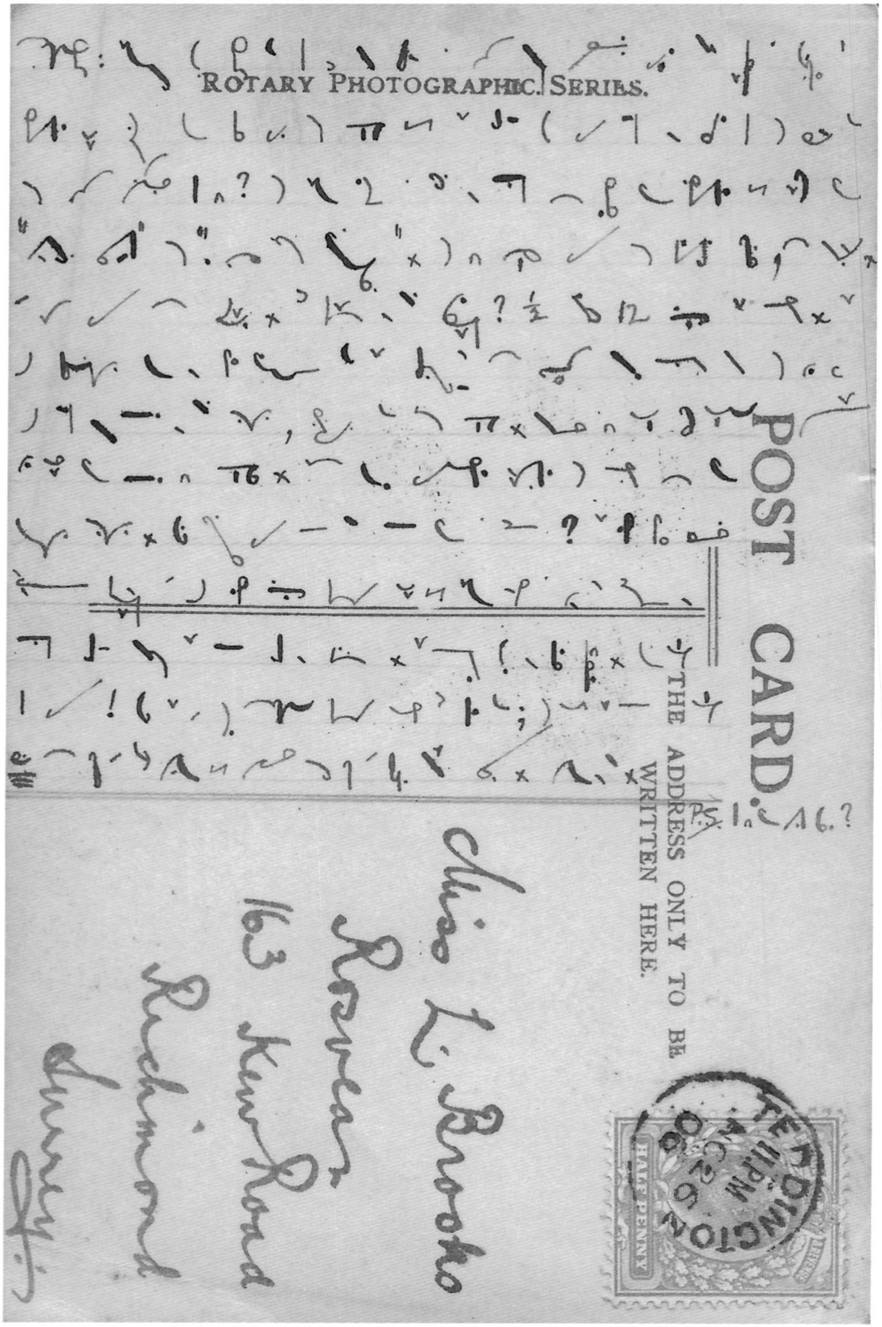
ROTARY PHOTOGRAPHIC SERIES.
POST CARD.
THE ADDRESS ONLY TO BE WRITTEN HERE.
P.S.
Miss L. Brooks
Rowena
163 Kew Road
Richmond
Surrey
TEDDINGTON
11 PM
06
HALF PENNY

This postcard of Castle Combe, sent by Percy to his sweetheart, contains the first part of a loving message and would have continued on another card. I have two more post-cards from Percy, but they do not follow on from this one. Transcribing place names can be tricky and the address at the top of this card is no exception. I have also found it impossible to fathom the name of the tablets Percy mentions later in the message.

Castle Combe. Renowned for being the prettiest place in Wiltshire. A Castle was built in the reign of Henry I of which only the dungeon remains. The Romans once occupied the place and traces of Saxon earthworks have been found.

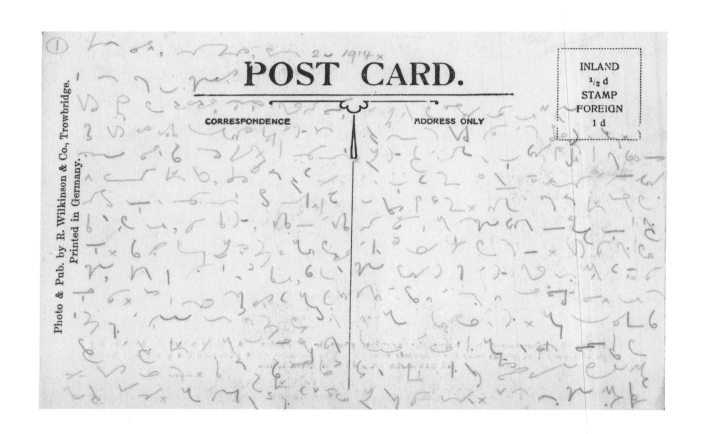

September 2nd 1914.

*Oh my very own darling one. Percy's sweetheart for always and always, my most precious little girl, dearest Percy wants to write you another few lines tonight and so I am making use of these cards which we purchased at Castle Combe. How quickly time passes, it seems hard to believe that our little plan to go to Castle Combe has been carried out and that it is all over now, still it is so, holidays come and holidays go. This last fact I shall not mind so much when I have you for always darling, it will be different later on to what it is now, that is if all goes well. I can't but mention my dearest one that I have been thinking of you oh so much today and longing in my heart so much for the happy blissful and peaceful time which I hope in God's providence will be our portion next year. It is hard to think of this time in the face of the present position of our country. I have longed to be with you today that I might comfort you and cheer you up for I expect you are unwell now and I long to be able to make your burdens lighter and your tasks easier to bear. I shall be so thankful and relieved to know that you are settled down at number 60 again and to know that work has become quite normal and regular and that you are not behind at all with the work. You will have a very hard time I expect for a little while but I hope my darling that you will be given strength to go on bravely and do what is necessary only for your good. Percy will pray for you darling for you are so dear and so precious to me and I hope that God will help you and bless you and keep you in His guardian care. Now my pet I have a few things to say. I have had another headache this afternoon and since tea I have taken two more * tablets for I think the two I took the day before yesterday were not sufficient and I think that I shall be better still tomorrow. I am improving darling and I feel decidedly ...*

LEARNING SHORTHAND

Repetition, repetition, repetition! Learning Pitman shorthand to a useful level demands daily practising, especially during the early months when covering the theory.

This postcard of two Japanese spaniels is written in poor quality Pitman and gives me the impression of somebody who is learning shorthand. The message shows that this is true:

84 Trafford Road
Salford
Dear Miss Beswick
  You will see by the above address that we have not yet removed. The house is not yet ready for us. They are painting it for us. Hoping you can read the shorthand (I have only just passed it). I remain
  Yours truly
  Lily Moffitt

C. W. FAULKNER & Co. LONDON, E.C.

DAI BUTZN. (JAPANESE SPANIELS.)

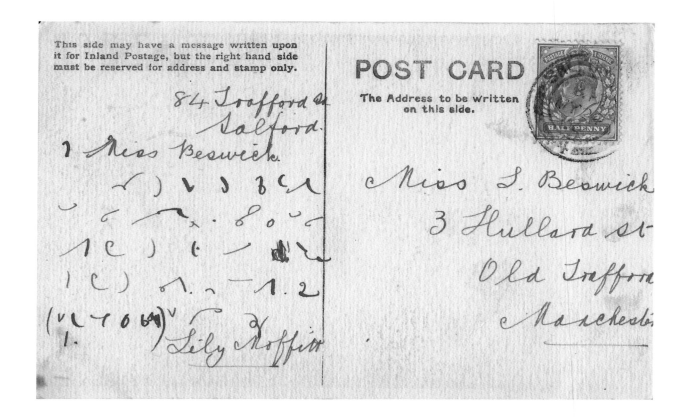

84 Trafford St
Salford.

Miss Beswick.

[shorthand notation]

Lily Moffitt

POST CARD

The Address to be written on this side.

HALF PENNY

Miss L. Beswick
3 Hullard St
Old Trafford
Manchester

Some messages specifically refer to learning shorthand. This postcard of four kittens was sent to the sender's two sisters who were on holiday on the Isle of Man:

Coventry 1913
Dear Winnie and May
    Thank you very much for your postcards. We are very glad to hear that you are having such a nice time. Allie is coming up tomorrow night to bring some of her things to put in the suitcase. We shall come by the afternoon boat and very likely on "Mona's Isle". Don't forget to look out for us. I am getting quite excited now. I am just going to my shorthand class so I can't stop to write any more. Daisy and Jessie have gone out. So goodbye, look out for us on Saturday.
    With love from Annie

Printed in Britain

Rotary Photo, London, E.C.

1913

Miss W. M. Cose.
c/o Mrs Callow.
Garthleigh
Broadway
Douglas.

Isle of Man

This 'official' postcard, complete with portrait of Sir Isaac Pitman, was sent by a shorthand teacher so, not surprisingly, the shorthand is textbook and beautifully written in ink:

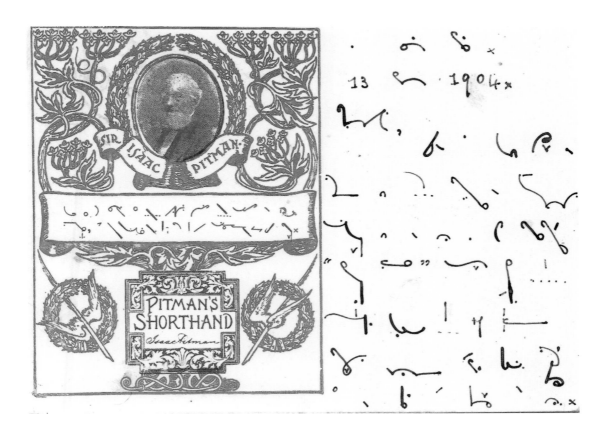

POST CARD

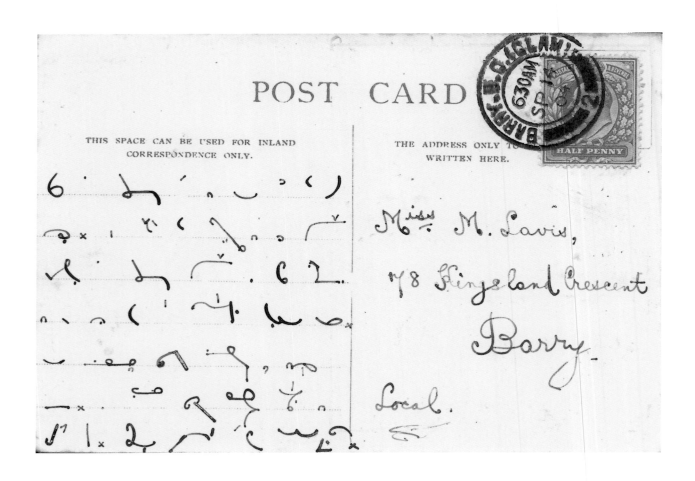

Miss M. Lavis,

78 Kingsland Crescent

Barry.

Local.

The same place.
13 September 1904.
Dear Martha,

    Just a few lines to ask you or perhaps to formally invite you to meet the other members of the proposed "speed class" in my study on Monday evening at 7 o'clock precisely to make and complete definite arrangements as to days and times of meeting.

The message on the address side is:

This is a postcard and you know what that usually means. But I thought that perhaps you would like to receive a postcard like the others asking you to meet them on Monday evening next. No excuse will be accepted, you must come. The class will not be successful unless you join it. There is no room for anything more. Jack

A postcard of Pitman's School on Southampton Row, London, shows young women in the 'fast' speed room. It was posted in 1909 and features an upside-down message. The sender did not foresee that the postmark would make the end of the message challenging to decipher.

PITMAN'S SCHOOL, SOUTHAMPTON ROW, LONDON.   "FAST" SPEED ROOM

20/7/09

Dear Frank

   Further to what I said to you yesterday Lizzie did speak to Emily about going on Friday and she said it would be quite convenient for her. The reason for this was that in the guide to Shanklin it said that excursions run on Fridays (and not Saturdays) at a rate something like 5/- per ticket less. So that would be worth considering would it not.

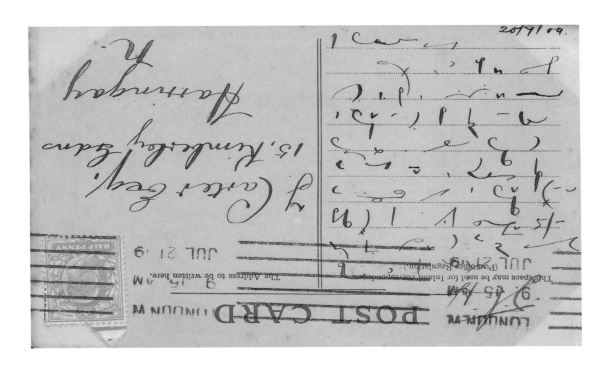

A popular theme for postcards was rough seas. This postcard of 'Boats in a Storm' at Scarborough, posted in 1904, is written in careful shorthand, with dotted lines written to show the correct position of some outlines. Pitman written like this often reveals a writer who is learning shorthand and the message confirms this:

SCARBOROUGH-BOATS IN A STORM.

Dear Lizzie

How are you getting on with your collection by this time? I have got 240 postcards. I have passed theory at last and I like speed very well so far. It seems rather funny going in the morning but I shall get used to that. How long are you supposed to be in speed before you get a situation? I wish I was out now. I wonder if I ever shall be?

With love and best wishes from Gladys.

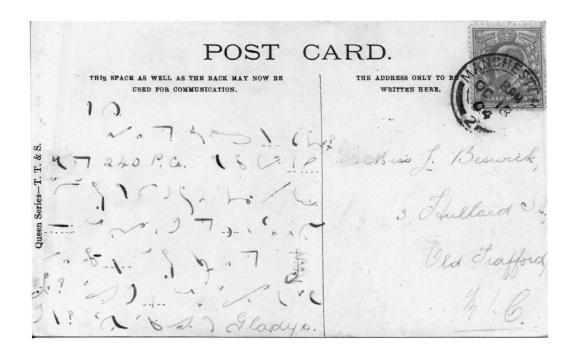

The postcard of 'His Private Secretary', complete with typed name and address of the recipient, has a message in carefully written shorthand. I strongly suspect this is from Miss Hole's shorthand and typing teacher.

"HIS PRIVATE SECRETARY."

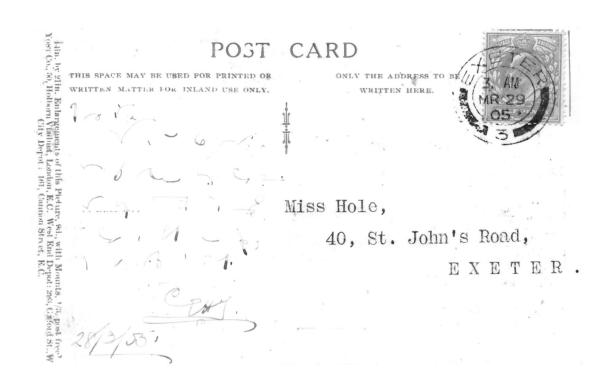

POST CARD

THIS SPACE MAY BE USED FOR PRINTED OR
WRITTEN MATTER FOR INLAND USE ONLY.

ONLY THE ADDRESS TO BE
WRITTEN HERE.

4in. by 21in. Enlargements of this Picture, 9d., with Mounts, 1/2, post free?
Yost Co., 50, Holborn Viaduct, London, E.C. West End Depot: 268, Oxford St., W.
City Depot: 161, Cannon Street, E.C.

28/3/05

Miss Hole,

    40, St. John's Road,

       E X E T E R .

Dear Miss Hole.

   Your letter to hand this morning. I am just leaving here for the week. I will therefore correct your exercises and forward on Saturday if possible, or at the latest on Monday.

   Yours faithfully

28/3/05

Practising shorthand at home, ideally every day, is essential for it to become automatic. In the message on this postcard of four kittens with 'The Governess', Lizzie has left it late before doing her homework:

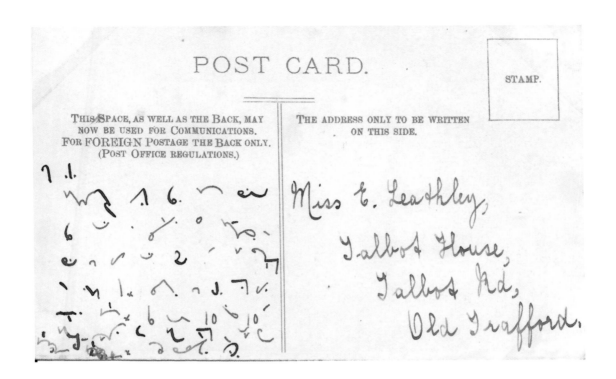

Dear Edie

    I hope you will be able to read this. I am sending this in a hurry as I promised to send you one in shorthand and I forgot all about it. Hoping you didn't get wet going home. It is now 10 past 10 and I have not done my letter that I have got tonight for homework.

    Yours sincerely, Lizzie

COLLECTING POSTCARDS

This postcard, 'Off to the Goodwins', was posted to a collector in New Zealand in 1908. Research into the writer reveals he was killed in action, aged 27, on 1 July 1916, the first day of the Battle of the Somme.

4 Aug 08
Dear Miss Toomey,
Here is another card for your collection. It is a view of the lifeboat being launched at Deal, where I have been staying for my holiday. We are having very fine weather here in England now, don't you wish you were here to enjoy it?
With kind regards
Please note I have changed my address
B J Devoil
The Retreat, Tower Hill,
Dorking, Surrey.

OFF TO THE GOODWINS.

Miss Muriel Toomey,
London St.,
Lyttelton.
N.Z.

(message in shorthand)

4 Aug '08.

B.G. Devoil,
The Retreat, Tower Hill,
Dorking, Surrey.

This Scottish clan postcard, posted in 1901, has the message written on the front because the reverse was reserved for the name and address at that time. It makes a polite but direct request for a postcard to add to a collection. The sender's shorthand is particularly beautiful and accurate:

151 High Park Road, Newcastle on Tyne November 23rd 1901.
Dear Arthur.

Would it be too much to ask you if you would send me a postcard of Tynemouth as I am collecting pictorial postcards and would like to increase my collection. Thanking you in advance I am yours very truly. James Wood.

This postcard of Newmarket Street, Falkirk, posted in 1904, implies that collecting postcards was a time-consuming hobby. The writer's shorthand is particularly neat and beautiful. She makes excellent use of phrasing – joining shorthand outlines together to save time and space.

Dear Miss Worthington.

Very many thanks for your kind Christmas card. I am very sorry I have been so long in replying but you will excuse me when I say that I am leaving Falkirk and have been very busy preparing. I have been appointed to a very good situation in a large engineering work over the Forth in a town called Alloa but my home is in Falkirk and my old address will still get me as I will be home for the weekends. I have so little time that I am afraid I will have to give up postcard collecting in the meantime but I will let you know next time how I am situated after I have tried my new situation.

With kind regards and yours sincerely
A C Paterson

Newmarket Street.   *Falkirk.*

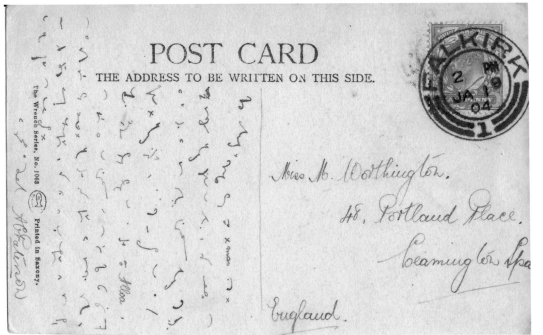

POST CARD

THE ADDRESS TO BE WRITTEN ON THIS SIDE.

The Wrench Series, No. 1063

Printed in Saxony.

FALKIRK
2 PM
JA 19
04
1

Miss M. Worthington,

48. Portland Place,

Leamington Spa

England.

Waterfall. Jesmond Dene, Newcastle

This postcard of 'Waterfall.
Jesmond Dene, Newcastle',
postmarked 31 May 1904,
in rather large shorthand,
is from another postcard
collector:

> *Was pleased to have your letter*
> *this morning and your postcard*
> *too. It is a nice one and so very*
> *clear. Tell Tom I am not done*
> *with postcards yet and will be*
> *so pleased if he will not think*
> *me very cheeky for telling you*
> *to tell him that.*
>
> > *Hope you like your room as*
> *well as the other.*
>
> > *Much love from Amy.*

A postcard of 'Scarborough North Bay and Pier' to Lizzie in 1904 has a newsy message with a final mention of the number of postcards that Gladys has in her collection. The message begins on the front:

SCARBOROUGH NORTH BAY & PIER

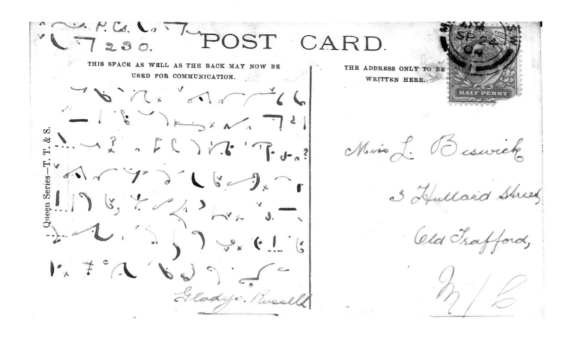

Dear Lizzie — You are quite a stranger now but I hope you are keeping in the best of health. I hope you will like this view and give it a place in your collection. How are you getting on with it by now? You start for your holidays on Monday, don't you? I hope you will enjoy yourself and have fine weather. My Dad had it very fine, only one shower all the time. I didn't go to see the wedding but I hear it was very nice. They had a fine day. With love and best wishes from a girl called Gladys Russell.

At the top it reads, 'How many postcards have you got now. I have got 230.'

LONGHAND AND SHORTHAND

Occasionally, a writer uses a mixture of longhand and shorthand. In this postcard of 'Young Rascals', the message starts in shorthand and includes a reference to the use of brandy, which the reader will understand. Then, longhand is squeezed into the remaining space with the addition of another 'secretive' sentence in shorthand which refers to 'Mabel'. I am not able to transcribe Mabel's surname.

Saturday evening, 6.30
My dear Frank,

*I received your 5th postcard last night, so I will forgive you, although I did not receive it in the morning. I had your letter by 1st post this morning, for which I thank you very much. I have just been indulging in some brandy, so you know what has started, but it does not come on very often. Mother gets down stairs now every day, but she cannot do much as she is so weak. Am glad you are enjoying yourself, and hope the change is doing you good. Are you getting any fatter? I have not been out this afternoon (only down the Street) as I have been keeping Mother company. Bertie has gone home for the weekend but he starts school again on Monday. I was rather surprised to hear you had tried Roller Skating, but why shouldn't you? As you can do so many things (except dance) I was sure you would be able to Roller Skate. Have you seen Mabel * yet? There is a great change in the weather here. Although it is nice and fine, it is very cold.*

Goodbye Babs, with love from E.m.e.w.

YOUNG RASCALS.

Six young rascals full of fun
Up to mischief, every one.

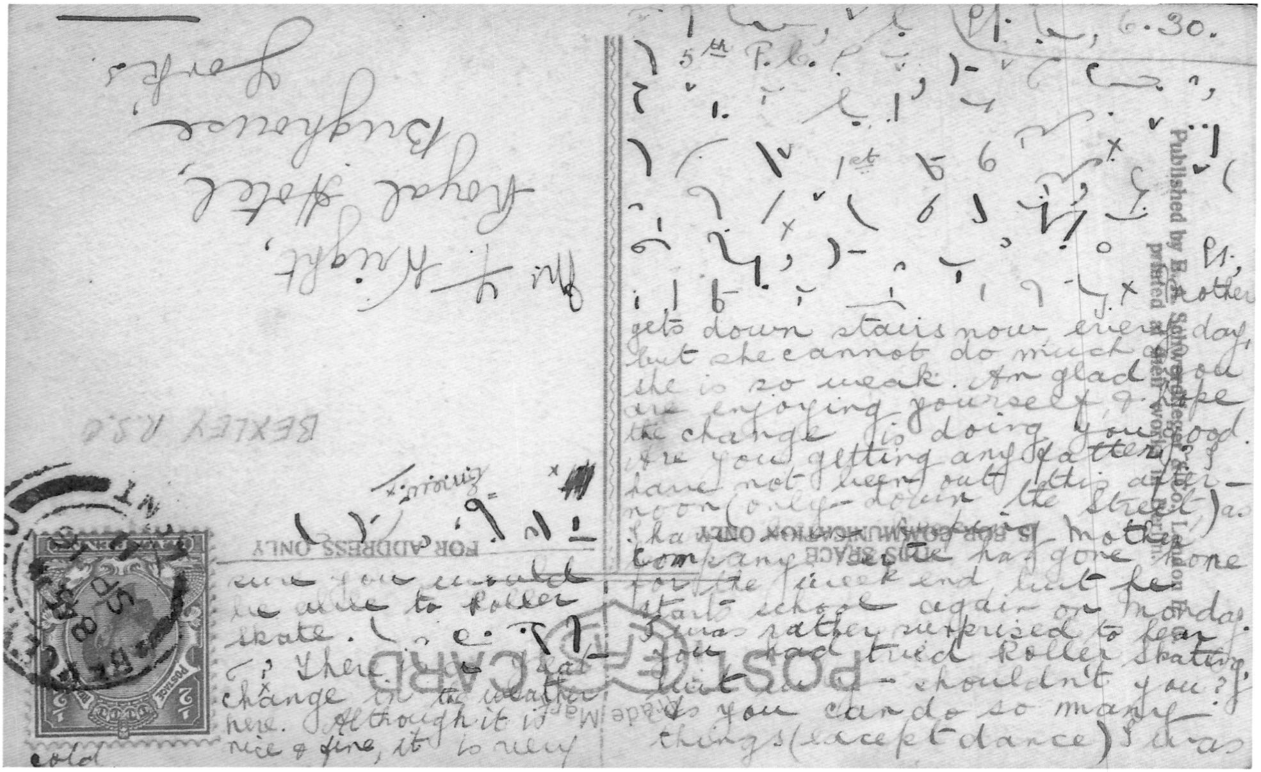

BEXLEY R.S.O.

[Address, written inverted:]
Miss M. Knight,
Royal Hotel,
Bexhill Park

[Message — right panel, partly in shorthand:]

5th F.b. ... 6.30

1st ...

P.S.

... gets down stairs now every day,
but she cannot do much as
she is so weak. Am glad you
are enjoying yourself & hope
the change is doing you good.
Are you getting any flatter?
Have not been out this afternoon (only down the street) as
I have ... Mother ...
company ... has gone home
for the week end but ...
starts school again on Monday.
I was rather surprised to hear
... had tried roller skating
... — shouldn't you? If
... you can do so many
things (except dance) I was

[Message — left panel:]

... you would
be able to roller
skate. ... There
change in the weather
here. Although it is
nice & fine, it is very
cold

Combining longhand and shorthand for secrecy is clear in the message on this postcard of actress Lily Brayton. But the writer has also taken advantage of shorthand in the last sentence, where she fits in an explanation of why she can no longer play the piano:

> *Excuse the card, but it is the only one I have. What must I do, of course you know I would much rather come to you on the 26th but if I don't go up to my future mother in law's she will be hurt ever so. I have written my boy asking him to get his mother to put others off until Tuesday and will let you know what they do. I hope they will do as I ask. Love from **
>
> *Don't expect me to play your piano because I shall not be able to play at all now having had no practice for a long time.*

Lily Brayton

"YES OR NO"
SERIES.

POST CARD.

This space, as well as the back, may be used for Inland Messages.

Excuse the card, but it is the only
one I have, What must I do,
of course you know I would
much rather come to you
on the 26th. but if I don't go
up to my [illegible]
she will be hurt ever so.
I have written [illegible]
[illegible]
[illegible]
[illegible] + Love from Sofa.
Don't expect me to play your piano because
[illegible]

The address only may be written here.

COVE[illegible] 8.30 PM DE 9 04

POSTAGE REVENUE HALF PENNY

Mme Bouveer
43 Lichfield St
Walsall

With a determination that the recipient would understand the message, longhand is used on the front of this postcard of Drake's Island: 'Hope to see you Monday'. The shorthand message on the reverse shows a degree of concern about whether it would be understood:

PLYMOUTH. DRAKE'S ISLAND FROM MOUNT EDGCUMBE.

Hope do see you Monday

Dear Maud,

 I hope you will like this card. I have been in this ruin. I hope you will understand this.
Nelly

ACTRESSES

Postcards of actresses were popular to collect. This one of American actress Billie Burke was posted in 1905. I am not sure of the sender's name, even though it is written in longhand.

62 Windley Street, Bolton
10.10.05
Dear Daisy
   Very pleased to inform you that I arrived home all right on Monday morning at 4 o'clock. I have not been very well since but I think my cold will be all right shortly. I still think you kept me out too late in the evenings Daisy but I would not mind some more walks all the same. Remember me to your father and mother. I hope your mother is getting better now.

The writer uses the top part of the card to fit in the last couple of sentences: 'Have you got anyone to carry your umbrella Daisy? Hope you will like this card. Yours sincerely **'.

SERIES 1389   MISS BILLIE BURKE.   DAVIDSON BROS. LONDON

This postcard of Camille Clifford has a slightly chiding message with a woeful lack of punctuation. I've added full stops to make it comprehensible:

Dear Len,
    Thank you very much for postcard. I think it is awfully pretty. I have never seen any like it before. I was very sorry to hear you were ill. Whatever is the matter with you? I thought nothing could be the matter with you. How dare you say it will be two years before you come to Manchester. I never heard such cheek. You told us when we were in Fog Lane with you that you could come at Christmas. Don't be long before you write again saying if you can come at Christmas.
    With best love
    Grace

HUTCHINSON & SVENDSEN

1778 P   MISS CAMILLE CLIFFORD.   ROTARY PHOTO. E.C

Mr L. Meakin
110 Edleston Road
Crewe

This postcard of the popular actress Marie Studholme has a message on both sides, written in particularly neat Pitman shorthand by Bert. On the front, the message reads: 'I think this is the position you said you would like. Is it? Bert'.

MISS MARIE STUDHOLME.

On the reverse Bert has written
a sweet message:

My dear little sweetheart,
    I hope you will like this one.
Last week this time I had the
great pleasure of taking you to
Ottery. What a difference now.
I trust that my dear little girl is
keeping quite well and that you
will not keep me too long without
a nice letter.
With much love and heaps
of kisses
    Bert

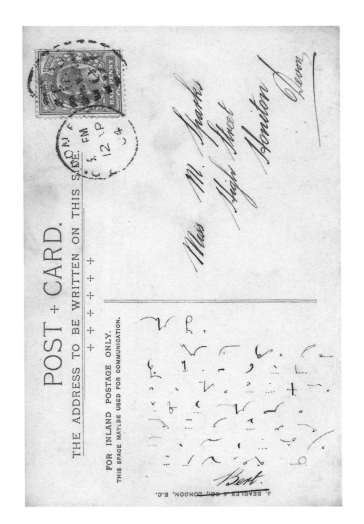

This postcard of a rural scene includes a Wordsworth quotation: '… Spring is there, hopeful and promising with buds and flowers.' The shorthand writer has added, 'The time for love and weddings.' On the reverse, the message points to postcard collecting, particularly ones of actresses:

" . . . SPRING IS THERE, *[shorthand]*
HOPEFUL AND PROMISING WITH BUDS AND FLOWERS."
Wordsworth.

16 Ansdell Road, Lytham, Lancs.
1 Sep 1908
Dear Elsie

Many thanks for nice actress received which I like very much. I am trying to get the <u>complete</u> set of Maud Allen as Salome so will you please send me some more of her. In return I will send anything you like. I only collect actresses now as I have so many views. I also collect foreign views from abroad. I have not had my photo taken yet but send you one I had taken by a friend of mine three years ago when I was 21 years of age. It is not a good one of me and of course I look a little older now but it will give an idea of what I look like. Write again soon and please send me an actress. If you cannot get Maud Allen I should like Adeline Genée.

Love from Henry

Jessie Bateman, an English stage actress, is pictured on this postcard from 1904.

So very many thanks for letter. I will write to you soon. This pen is too thick for shorthand. I do hope your brother is quite better. It is pouring cats and dogs. When do the classes for the next session begin. If I had been at the swimming baths the first time you would have gone in.
     With love from Edie.

MISS JESSIE BATEMAN.

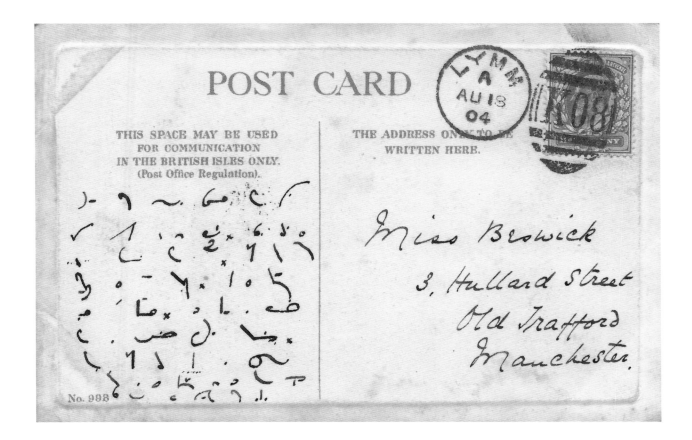

POST CARD

THE ADDRESS ONLY TO BE
WRITTEN HERE.

LYMM
A
AU 18
04

K08

No. 998

Miss Broswick
3, Hulland Street
Old Trafford
Manchester.

A postcard of Gabrielle Ray has this sentence written in longhand: 'Is not the overleaf a beautiful one and a charming picture'. The shorthand message is chummy and written with warmth by Bessie to 'darling' Dora, yet starts, 'My dear Miss Dickinson':

13/6/05
My dear Miss Dickinson.

Thanks very much for card received yesterday morning. I have not been able to write before as my head has been very bad since I left school last Friday. I am trying to enjoy myself, and have many invitations out but am not able to fulfil all of them. Please tell me if you can understand my shorthand. I have still got that pretty card of Gertie Millar and will send it soon. I like the one you sent me and hope you will like this one in return Dora. My head is very much against my enjoying my holiday but I sincerely hope dear you are enjoying yourself. It is so nice to receive cards from someone. It does liven me up and especially when they are from you darling. Once again hoping you will like this one and remain yours very truly.

Bessie

PHILCO SERIES 3075 D   GABRIELLE RAY.

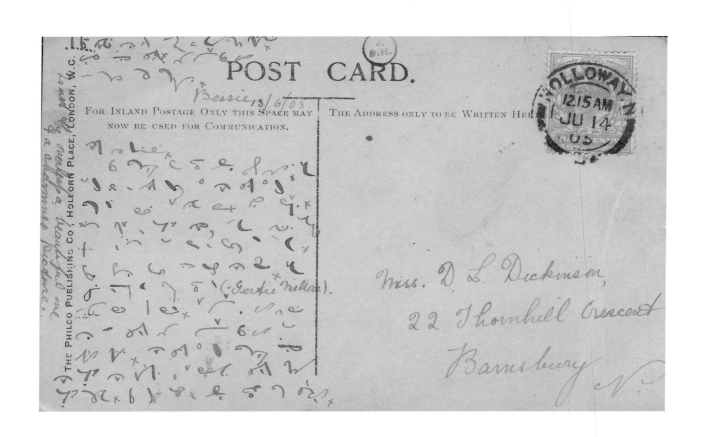

POST CARD.

FOR INLAND POSTAGE ONLY THIS SPACE MAY NOW BE USED FOR COMMUNICATION.

THE ADDRESS ONLY TO BE WRITTEN HER[E]

Bessie 13/6/03.

(Gertie Millar).

Miss D. L. Dickinson,
22 Thornhill Crescent
Barnsbury
N.

MYSTERIES

This postcard of Fairy Glen, Bettws-y-coed, is from an unnamed sender. It is written in idiosyncratic Pitman and has a tantalisingly mysterious message:

Fairy Glen, Bettws-y-coed.

London February 20 1905
  This is known as "Lovers Glen", as so many proposals have taken place here. Have not been myself, so was not caught. But I know of a place which is quite as fairy-like to me.

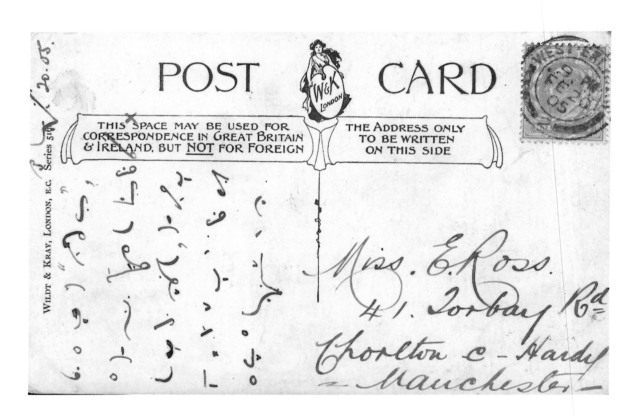

Harry sent the following photographic postcard of 'Inspection Car Normanton Oct 20th 1906' to Sidney in 1909. Although difficult to make out, Harry has marked an 'X' on it and refers to this in the message. The postcard is very grubby and creased but still provides a useful slice of social history. What does Harry mean by his postscript?

Dear Sidney

I am sorry I have not written before, you must try to excuse me. I received your letter but was ill when I got it. I hope you are enjoying your holidays, I think I am. Can you see who that is below the cross. I see Jeffries is going to fight Johnson.

Your old chum

Harry

PS "Oh yes"

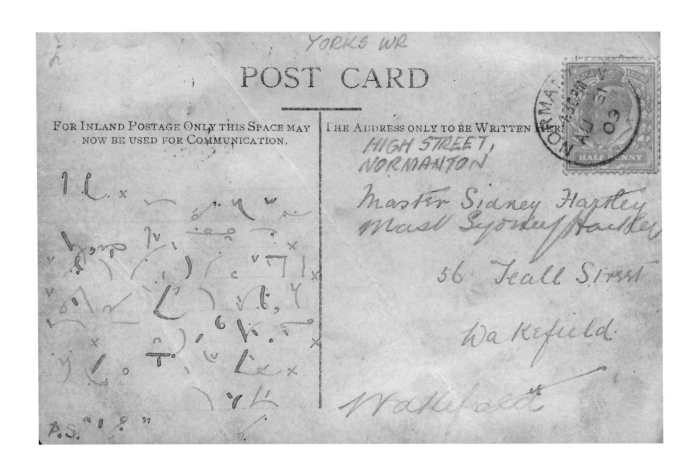

YORKS WR

POST CARD

HIGH STREET,
NORMANTON

Master Sidney Hartley

56 Teall Street

Wakefield

P.S. "⌐ ⌐ "

FINAL WORD

Use it or lose it! Pitman shorthand needs to be used regularly or the writer is in danger of forgetting it. This postcard of Lymm Cross and Stocks, posted in 1904, has a plaintive message from Edie about her mistakes. Three of her shorthand outlines have confounded me.

The message on the front is: 'Would you mind telling me my mistakes please. Read your letter in shorthand. The cross has been taken from here and a weather vane put up.'

Lymm Cross and Stocks   Valentines Series

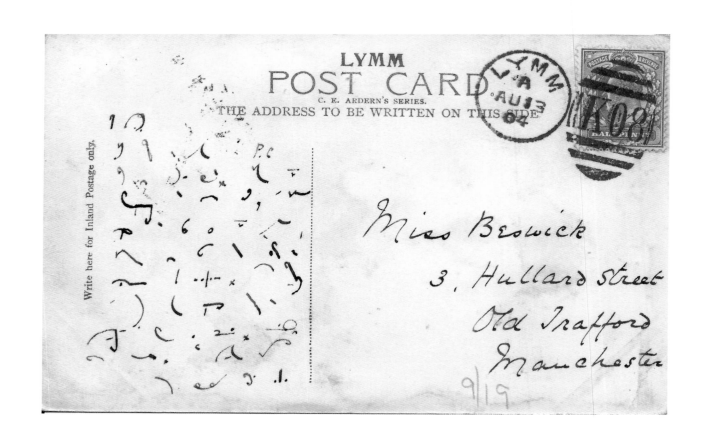

LYMM

POST CARD

C. E. ARDERN'S SERIES.

THE ADDRESS TO BE WRITTEN ON THIS SIDE

Write here for Inland Postage only.

Miss Beswick

3, Hullard Street

Old Trafford

Manchester

The back reads:

Dear Lizzie

I was surprised to receive a postcard from you so soon. I have quite forgotten all my shorthand, and I know most of this is quite wrong but I hope you will be able to make it out. My brother and sister have gone up to London for a week. ***

With love I remain

Your sincere friend Edie

Edie's message in less-than-perfect shorthand lives again. I aim to preserve the tiny stories on postcards, by transcribing their Pitman shorthand messages. Thank you to all those who wrote their messages on these fifty picture postcards over 100 years ago. And to those who received and treasured them – thank you.

ACKNOWLEDGEMENTS

Thank you to my friend, Gill Hall, who has helped me transcribe some incredibly challenging Pitman shorthand. Any errors in transcription are entirely mine.

For the past five years, it has been a pleasure to share some of my postcards with my followers on Twitter (@Kathryn11Baird). They have proved that Pitman shorthand continues to be useful, beautiful and interesting.

Thank you to Amy Rigg and her colleagues at The History Press for their fascination with my niche hobby and their commitment to bringing these mysterious messages to a wider audience.

Finally, thank you to my son Tom and husband Robert for their support and encouragement.

All of the postcards in this book are from the author's collection.